THE
KABBALA

THE
KABBALA

An Introduction to Jewish Mysticism and Its Secret Doctrine

Dr. Erich Bischoff

WEISERBOOKS
Boston, MA/York Beach, ME

First published in 1985 by
Red Wheel/Weiser, LLC
York Beach, ME
With offices at
368 Congress Street
Boston, MA 02210
www.redwheelweiser.com

First published in Germany circa 1910

Library of Congress Catalog Card Number: 84-52262
ISBN 0-87728-564-0
BJ

Cover art is a mezuzah from the Jewish Museum, London. This photograph of
the 15th century Italian bone carving is used by kind permission of the Warburg
Institute, London.

Typeset in 11 point Perpetua

Printed in the United States of America

08 07 06 05 04 03
15 14 13 12 11 10 9 8 7 6

The paper used in this publication meets the minimum requirements of the
American National Standard for Permanence of Paper for Printed Library
Materials Z39.48-1984.

TABLE OF CONTENTS

LIST OF FIGURES

FOREWORD

For centuries, reflective people have felt attracted to the lonely path of mysticism. Since ancient times this path existed and it was not the most common of minds that searched for it. The paths of mysticism have been many and varied, but all have aimed at one goal: the ONE that contains ALL! Not only to Rome lead many roads; it would be a mistake to consider but one single way as the only true one. Although many students of mysticism have explored Buddhism, the Kabbala and its doctrines have a long and profound history as well. Mystics as well as those people who are aware of the development of the human spirit throughout the ages have studied Kabbala. It is even possible that the Kabbalistic line of thought is deeper than that of the Buddhistic.

In spite of excellent work exploring this field there is still no book that, short and easily understandable to everyone, provides the reader with material that is worth knowing from the Kabbala. Because of this, I have used a question and answer format to try to impart the most remarkable information from the Kabbala, believing that Jewish literature is still much closer to us than that of the orient. For those readers to whom this subject is new, I hope that this book will not be a disappointment. The illustrations come, for the greater part, from very rare originals that were very difficult to come by.

The Author

THE KABBALA

CHAPTER 1

CHARACTER AND ORIGIN OF THE KABBALA

1. What is the Kabbala?

The Kabbala contains the complete mystical doctrines of Judaism which include the theosophical-metaphysical-naturalistic speculations as well as the fantasies based upon magical superstitions.

2. What does Kabbala actually mean?

This name, in use since the 13th century A.D., really means *tradition*. The system can lay claim to the name "secret doctrine" insofar that it was known (other than to Bible and Talmud scholars) to only a very few. It was communicated to excellent pupils only.

3. How old is the Kabbala?

The Kabbalists date the principle conceptions of the Kabbala back to the earliest times—back to Moses and even to Abraham and Adam. As to the true founders of the Kabbala, however, they mention mainly three Talmudists: Rabbi Ismael ben Elisa (about 130 A.D.), Rabbi Nechunjah ben Hakana (about 75 A.D.), and especially Simeon ben Yohai (about 150 A.D.), the last of whom they point out is author of the famous *Zohar* (see also question 45).

Figure 1. Rabbi Simeon ben Yohai.

4. How much of the Kabbala should be believed?

Such speculations as the Kabbala contains are in general foreign to the nature of the older Judaism and especially to the original Mosaism. The enormous collective work, the *Talmud,* does contain many mystical conceptions about God and his chariot (the "Merkabah" according to Ezekiel); about heaven, hell, and the world (angelology, demonology, cosmology); about the origin, character, and the continual existence of the soul; the future world; and about various magical rituals. Some of these contemplations and rituals are, nevertheless, often classified as risky, useless, and dangerous. The elements entering mostly from Persia and later from Neoplatonism have nothing to do with the character of the Talmud writings. Such speculations and doctrines are not communicated by the three above-mentioned Talmud scholars (see question 3) even though they exist within the *Talmud* of Midrasch. The Kabbala as a mystical system—and its development as such—belongs undoubtedly in the Middle Ages and its origin dates at most back to the 7th century A.D. From then on it richly developed in various ways until it reached its peak in the book *Zohar* (see question 45), with its last offshoots extending to our time.

5. Which periods can be distinguished in the development of Kabbalism?

1. Its origin up to the book *Yetsirah.*
2. Its further development under the influence of the book *Yetsirah* (10th-12th century).

3. The completion of the Kabbala from the rise of the actual Sephiroth system to the end of the book *Zohar* (13th-15th century).
4. The later development (16th-17th century).
5. The fall (since the 18th century).

6. Is the Kabbala based on oral tradition only?

No. Several of its doctrines may have been propagated for a long time only orally before they were written down; others may not have been communicated in writing. But what we know of the Kabbala comes from written sources and the first certain knowledge about the Kabbalistic doctrines was drawn exclusively from the Kabbalistic writings dating from the 7th-9th century.

7. Is the Kabbalistic literature extensive?

Very extensive. In addition to a great number of printed writings there exists in public and private libraries an unbelievable amount of manuscripts of Kabbalistic nature which are hardly known. Furthermore one supposes that many more such writings have been lost.

8. In which language is this literature written?

Mainly in new Hebrew and Chaldean, like the *Talmud* literature. Only a few commentaries on the book *Yetsirah* (see question 17) are written in Arabic.

9. Which Kabbalistic book is written in Chaldean?

The *Zohar*, written in Spain at the end of the 13th century, the principal work of Kabbalistic literature.

10. What are the contents of the Kabbalistic writings?

In addition to theosophical, metaphysical, cosmological, naturalistic, and other such speculations, and in addition to daring poetical representations of abstract ideas and high ethical thoughts, there is also systemically arranged nonsense, worthless fantasies, and various superstitions.

11. Which three main schools of thought can be distinguished in Kabbalism?
The metaphysical-speculative, the ethical-ascetical, and the magical-superstitious, though they cannot be clearly distinguished. The decline of Kabbalism in more modern times is mainly charaterized by an emphasis on the latter.

12. How was and is the attitude of Judaism as such toward Kabbalism?
Until the 9th century, the Talmudic Jews held a hostile attitude toward Kabbalism. In the 10th century it was the authority of the Gaon Saadja (892-942 A.D.), the famous founder of Hebrew linguistic research in relation to Kabbalism, who obtained followers amongst rabbis. In the 12th and 13th century their number was growing mainly because of the example of the famous Talmud scholars Nachmanides and Gikatilla (see question 30). During the 17th century Judaism as a whole was under the influence of the Kabbala. In the 18th century respect for the Kabbala declined under the influence of the era, and modern Judaism considers the Kabbala as not much more than a historical curiosity or subject for literary historical research.

CHAPTER 2

HISTORY OF THE KABBALA

13. What are the characteristics of the first period of Kabbalism?
Instead of the later more speculative tendency, the religious fantasy was dominant during this period.

14. What is the principal subject of the mystical doctrine of this period?
The mysteries of the Godhead and the kingdom of heaven with its hosts, especially the glory of God throned (see question 4), and the activities of the archangel Metatron, as well as the other heavenly beings, and finally the exaltation to the mystical intuition of these matters.

15. What are the main works from this period?
1. *Othijoth de Rabbi Akiba* (the alphabet by Rabbi Akiba) in which the separate letters of the Hebrew alphabet are given a religious, moral, and mystical-fantastic nature.
2. *Schiûr Komah* (determination of the greatness of the divine nature) wherein on the sections that were preserved, the greatness of the

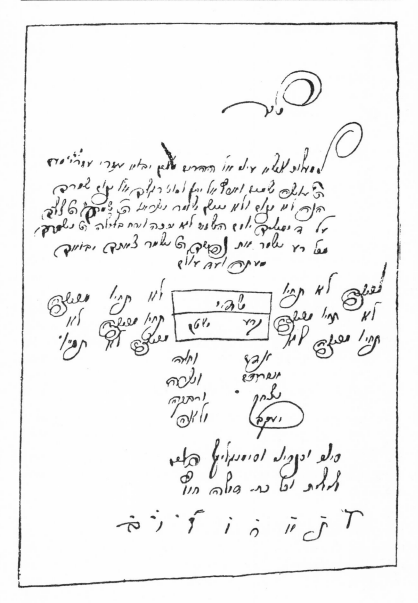

Figure 2. From the *Gaon Hai*.

anthropomorphized Godhead is described. This fantastic sequence of numbers has been meant allegorically but the profound meaning is hardly to be unravelled.

3. *Hechaloth Rabbathi* (the great treatise on heavenly halls) presents information about methods for attaining mystical ecstasy and describes that which one sees during this ecstasy.

16. Are there more Kabbalistic books known from this period?

Yes. The *Gaon Hai* (see Figure 2), for example, mentions writings of magical content dealing with amulets and magical formulas by means of which one could still storms at sea, inspire love, kill people, etc.; and also *Sepher ha-jaschar, Sepher ha-rasim, Sepher Schêm ben Noach,* all of which however have been lost.

17. How can the second period of Kabbalism be distinguished from the first?

In the *Sepher Yetsirah* (the Book of Formation) it is not so much described theosophically but rather more cosmologically. Its subject is the beginning and the active elements of the world of apparitions; it becomes more and more speculatively-systematical. Later the cosmological and theosophical direction unite—especially with the Jewish mystics in Germany about the beginning of the 13th century—developing an ethic embued with mysticism of the most noble kind. Also, a letter mysticism with a magical purpose more emphasized came out of the theosophical speculation about place and numbers of the letters in the names of God and the angels, prayer words, etc.

18. What are the fundamental thoughts of the book *Yetsirah*?

As the words and those things expressed by words form (in the view of this author) an inseparable whole the elements of the words (namely the 22 letters of the Hebrew alphabet) are also the elements of the things expressed. Above them stand, as categories of all that exists, the numbers of the first decade (1-10) that present a closed entity. The highest principal is the absolute unity above each number.

19. In what way did the world develop out of this absolute unity according to the book *Yetsirah*?

The unity is represented by the number 1: this is the breath (spirit) of the living God. From this originates the 2, "the Spirit of spirits," the voice in which the 22 letters as elements of things come into being; physically this breath represents the air. Out of the 2 develops the 3, or out of the air develops the primeval water of chaos, out of which water and earth separate. Out of the 3 develops the 4, or out of the primeval water the primeval fire, as fire in connection with air and water procreates heaven and its inhabitants. Next to these four elementary numbers come the 6 elementary dimensions (height, depth, eastern, western, northern, and southern direction) which form with the others the elementary decade which contains all categories of creation. When the 22 letters connect with the 10 numbers or fundamental principals, the isolated things come into being. As this connection is cyclical[1] however, these things repeatedly change. The circumstances under which this complete development takes place are subject to law, opposite laws, and mediation (thesis, antithesis, and synthesis).

20. What is one reminded of in this cosmogony with its number principles?

Of the striking resemblance of the doctrines of the Greek Neopythagoreans.

21. When was the book *Yetsirah* written?

According to some, in the 8th or 9th century A.D. In all probability, however, at the end of the 9th or the beginning of the 10th century. Some regard the Gaon Saadja, the founder of Hebrew linguistics who first wrote his commentaries in Arabic in 931, as the author of this book (written in Hebrew) mainly because the perfection of the letters and its classification seem to point to him. In addition many others

---

[1]Compare the tuning (but physical) atoms of Democritus. It is noteworthy that the monad theory through which van Helmont preceded Leibniz originated from the Kabbalistic point of view. His monads, like those of Leibniz, are animated in the Kabbala.

wrote commentaries on this important work referring to the theosophical Kabbala.

22. What makes the book *Rasiêl* more remarkable than the others?

It is a certain transition from the cosmological tendency of the book *Yetsirah* to the pure theosophical direction, while it points out the close connection that exists between the supernatural and the mundane world. In particular this book provides information about the influence of the stars on human destiny so that man through this science is able to unveil the future. By way of this it introduces astonomy, or better astrology, into the Kabbalistic doctrine (see question 202).

23. Could you mention two representatives of the German ethical-mystical school of thought from the second period?

Rabbi Juda ben Samuel ha-Chafid, the author of the excellent moralistic writings *Sepher chasidim* (the Book of the Pious), who died in Regensburg in 1217; and a pupil, Rabbi Eleasar ben Juda (also called "Rokêach" after his main work), who died in Worms in 1237. He (Eleasar) developed the letter mysticism in his commentaries on the book *Yetsirah*. [2]

24. What is the main characteristic of the third period of Kabbalism?

The doctrine of the 10 "Sephiroth" and its influence on the further doctrines of Kabbalistic speculation.

25. What is to be understood by "Sephiroth"?

"Sephiroth" is the plural of "Sephirah." Actually it is the Greek "spheres" but in Hebrew it also means "number." Corresponding to the 10 spheres of Ptolemaic astronomy and the 10 "numbers" of the book *Yetsirah* (see question 19), "Sephiroth" stands for 10 active

---

[2]His name (Eleasar) and the title of his main work (*Rokeach*) have the same numerological value and are therefore, according to the Gematria (see question 37, page 11), replaceable. "Rokeach" means pharmacist.

primeval ideas or metaphysical primeval forces which represent the mediation between the absolute Godhead and the whole world.

26. Were there other names for the Sephiroth?

In the first period they were sometimes called "Maamrim," meaning "conditions of creation," because it is stated in the Talmud that the world was created with ten words. This expression also means "categories" as is the case with the 10 fundamental numbers (Sephiroth) of the book Yetsirah; the meaning soon changes into the conception "creative primeval thought."

27. Do the Sephiroth from the third period differ from the previous periods?

Yes; also their subdivisions have completely different names. Whereas "primeval numbers" represent abstract cosmological ideas, "primeval conceptions" are of a metaphysical nature.

28. Who is considered the founder of the Sephiroth doctrine?

Rabbi Isaac the Blind (about 1200 A.D.) from Nîmes in Provence.

29. Which Kabbalistic book comes out of this period?

Sepher Bahîr (the Book of Light), a writing that is very mysterious, contrary to its title.

30. Could you mention some other famous Kabbalists from the third period?

Asrièl ben Menachem, a pupil; Ascher ben David, a cousin of Isaac the Blind; Mose ben Nachman (Nachmanides, 1195-1270 A.D.); Todros (ben Joseph Ha-Lewi) Abulafia (second half of the 13th century); Abraham Abulafia (1240-1282); Joseph (ben Abraham) Gikatilla (born 1248); and Mose (ben Schem tob) de Leon (1250-1305).

31. What can be said about the first two Kabbalists?

They were dedicated to the dialectical development of the Sephiroth doctrine that was previously propagated dogmatically.

32. For what reason is Nachmanides important to Kabbalism?
He is believed to have written the commentary on the *Sepher Yetsirah*
which, however, is credited as the work of Asriêl. He was of even
greater importance because, being the greatest *Talmud* authority of his
time, he added in his much-read commentaries on the *Five Books of
Moses,* Kabbalistic interpretations and doctrines.

**33. What is the contribution of Todros Abulafia to the
Kabbala?**
He was the prime instigator of the doctrine of the (ten) Kelippôth,
meaning "shell" or "cover," or of the physical elements out of the
world of apparitions which correspond to the (ten) Sephiroth of the
supernatural world, and which relate to each other in a similar way as
Plato said material things relate to thoughts.

34. What makes Abraham Abulafia remarkable?
In addition to the Sephiroth doctrine he also successfully propagated
letter mysticism as well as the Kabbalistic treatment of the names of
God, which he considers the goal of secret science.

35. What are the principal methods of this letter Kabbalism?
Gematria, Notarikon, and Themurah.

36. What is meant by Gematria?
Gematria (geometry) is the replacement of a meaningful word in a
bible verse, etc., either by another whose letters have the same numerological value,[3] or by a conception to which the corresponding letter
is related.

37. What are a few examples of this method?
In the *First Book of Moses* (Chapter 49 verse 10) it states: Ad Ki Jabo
Schiloh (until Schiloh comes). The letters in "Jabo Schiloh" have the
numerological value of 348 in Hebrew. The letters in "Maschîach"

---

[3]The first ten letters of the Hebrew alphabet correspond to the numbers 1-10, the
eleventh through the nineteenth letters to the numbers 20-100, the twentieth through
the twenty-second letters to the numbers 200-400.

(messiah) have the same numerological value. This word is for clarifying the obscurity "Schiloh" puts in a verse and gives it a messianac meaning.[4] Also, in *Habicok* (Chapter 3, verse 2) is stated: "In wrath remember mercy" (Rachem). The numerological value of "Rachem" is 248. Therefore the 248 positive commandments of the Mosaic law are meant.[5]

38. What is meant by Notarikon?

Notarikon (from notariacum, meaning abbreviation) is the treating of the letters of a word as the first letters of a sentence or group of sentences. In other words, the treatment of a seemingly important word as a secret abbreviation.

39. What would be a few examples of this?

In *"Gan Eden"* or *Garden of Eden, First Book of Moses* (Chapter 2 verse 8) the basic letters (G N E D N) are considered to be the first letters of the words Guph, Nèphesch, Ezem, Dàath, Nèzach (Body, Soul, Bones, Knowledge, Eternity). In this way the "Garden of Eden" in which man was placed takes the meaning from the nature of the earth consisting of body and immortal soul. The word "Abiad" or Father of eternity, *Isaiah* (Chapter 2 verse 5) is explained by the Kabbalists as Azilah, Beriah, Yetsirah, Asijjah, Daleth (emanation, creation, formation, making). Letter D is 4, the indication of the 4 worlds that develop out of the absolute, and the one out of the other.

40. What is meant by Themurah?

The replacement of the letters of a meaningful word, or a word that needs explanation in such a way that a new word originates.

41. What are some examples of this?

In *Psalms 21* (verse 1) it is stated: "The King shall joy in thy strength, oh Lord." Which king is meant becomes clear through the replace-

---

[4]See also question 23. "Eleasar" is "Rokeach"

[5]Compare also the cynical reference in Hebrew to a pharmacist as a "ninety-niner," meaning "the man who earns 99%," because the Hebrew letters for "pharmacist" have the numerological value of 99.

ment of the letters of "jismach"; that way one gets "maschiach," meaning messiah. In the *Second Book of Moses* (Chapter 23 verse 23) it is stated: "My angel (meleachi) shall cometh unto thee." By replacement of the letters (Themurah) the Kabbalist discovers that the angel Michael is meant.

42. Are there still more such methods?

Yes. For instance "Ziruph" (letter transposition), the interchange of all or some letters of a word by certain others. For instance, the replacement of the first letter (Aleph) by the last (22nd) letter of the alphabet (Thêt), or of the second (Beth) by the 21st (Schin), or of the third by the 20th. This is the A T H B (A) S C H according to the following scheme:

```
 11 10  9  8  7  6  5  4  3  2  1

{ כ  ׳  ט  ח  ז. ו. ה. ר. ג  ב  א }
{ ל  מ  נ  ס  ע  פ  צ. ק  ר  ש  ת }

 12 13 14 15 16 17 18 19 20 21 22
```

This way new words or number words originate that can, in addition, be treated according to the Gematria (see question 36).

43. Can you tell us some examples of this?

In *Jeremiah* (Chapter 25 verse 26) it is stated: "And the King of Shéshach"; by the method of transposition "Athbasch" one gets for "shéshach" the word "Babel." Consequently the king of Babel is meant. In the *First Book of Moses* (Chapter 38 verse 29) "Pèrez" is mentioned; according to the letter transposition "Athbasch" one gets the letters that have the same numerological value 14 (see question 36). The word "David" has the same numerological value. Therefore "Pèrez" secretly means David. In the *Fourth Book of Moses* (Chapter 7 verse 14) the word "Ketòreth" is mentioned. The first letter of "Ketòreth" becomes, according to the Athbasch, a 4, so the numerological value of the word becomes 613; this same numerological value is found for all Ten Commandments so that "Ketòreth" secretly means law enforcement. In the same way the different letter methods are even further combined and complicated.

44. Was the influence of letter mysticism far reaching?
Yes; Gikatilla wrote about it in his influential works and was so successful with it that this letter mysticism or artificial Kabbala was often regarded as the main part of Kabbalism.

45. For what reason is Moses de Leon remarkable?
He had an exceptional knowledge of the mystical Kabbalistic literature and is in all probability the author of the book *Zohar* (meaning Splendid), the culmination point of the Kabbala. To make the work more respected he ascribed it to the famous Talmudist Simeon ben Yohai (see question 3) and presented himself only as a discoverer of the book.

46. When was the *Zohar* written?
Its oldest parts date from the end of the 13th century A.D.

47. Is it complete in itself?
No. It consists of an older part in the form of a Midrasch (meaning far-reaching statement) about the *Five Books of Moses*, and also of parts of another nature of younger date which are, however, based in general on the same principles.

48. Name a few of those other parts!
Sifra-di-Tseniuta (the book of the veiled mystery), *Idra rabba* (greater assembly), *Idra Zuta* (lesser assembly), *Raaja mehemna* (the true shepherd),[6] *Tikkunê Zohar* (amendments to the *Zohar*), *Zohar Hadash*, (*the New Zohar*).

49. Which part is the oldest?
Sifra-di-Tseniuta. The youngest is undoubtedly the *Zohar Hadash*, which is made up of different sections. The age of the other parts is hard to determine.

---

[6]The name for Moses as well as Christ in the New Testament.

50. When and where was the *Zohar* first published?
In 1558 in Cremona in a folio edition. Later it was published with a different text order in Mantua in 1558-1560 in a quarto edition. The later editions come very close to this one even in relation to the numbering of pages (see question 18). Figure 3 on page 16 shows the title page of one edition.

51. How does the *Zohar* relate to present-day Kabbalism?
It unites all its sections (in an often fantastic way) into one large entity that in its individual parts, however, is badly arranged.

52. Does it come up with something really new?
What is new is that the method of the arrangement of thesis and antithesis by way of third principal (Thesis, Antithesis, Synthesis), which in the book *Yetsirah* was only applied to cosmogony (see question 19), now becomes an actual solid factor for the complete metaphysics. In other words, the complete emanation process is explained by the working of these three principals. Especially new is the presentation of the metaphysical priority and contrast between a male and a female principle (father and mother), whose polarity is neutralized by a third mediating principle (son).

53. Didn't Gikatilla already make a distinction between a male and a female principle in the working of the Sephiroth?
Metaphorically he did describe the (in his opinion) more receptive (passive) Sephiroth as feminine and the more productive (active) as masculine but he did not systematically develop this conception; it is only in the *Zohar* that "the son" as principle of the synthesis of the masculine and feminine is actively and ambiguously brought in.

54. How does the *Zohar* represent these three principles?
The masculine by the letter Jôd, by the name of God (Jhwh) and also by the color white; the feminine by the letter Hê and the color red; the mediating principle (son) by the letter Wâw and the color green.[7]

---

[7]Green is the middle color of the rainbow. Red is the most powerful color, and white is colorless.

KABBALÆ DENUDATÆ

TOMUS SECUNDUS:

Id eſt

LIBER

SOHAR

RESTITUTUS;

Cujus contenta pagina verſa monſtrabit.

OPUS

Omnibus genuinæ antiquitatis, & ſublimio-
rum Hebraicæ gentis dogmatum indagatoribus, nec non
Hebraicæ & Chaldaicæ linguæ, & in ſpecie Idiomatis Terræ Iſraeliticæ,
tempore Chriſti & Apoſtolorum uſitati, Studioſis, aliisque curioſis
utiliſſimum, & vere Kabbaliſticum.

cui adjecta

Adumbratio Cabbalæ Chriſtianæ ad captum Judæorum.

FRANCOFVRTI,

Sumptibus JOANNIS DAVIDIS ZUNNERI.

Typis BALTHASAR. CHRISTOPH. WUSTII Sen. 1684.

Figure 3. Title page of one edition of the *Zohar*.

55. Have Christian ideas had any influence on these fundamental principles?

If they did, their influence was very limited and at least not in a special Christian form. The Trinity which some for the sake of the messianac mission would like to find in the *Zohar* is even in a form which shows Christian mysticism very different from the trinity principle of the Kabbala. In the Christian Trinity the "Father" represents darkness, severity, revengefulness; the "Son," which emanates from him, represents light and compassion; and the "Spirit," originating from both, represents the merciful, all-encompassing principle, whereas in the *Zohar* the "Father" represents patience, the "Mother" severity, and the "Son" preserving mercifulness. The Neoplatonic speculations that reached the Jewish authors through Arabic translations of the original Greek writings have definitely had the greatest influence.

56. What other remarkable doctrine is favored by the *Zohar*?

The doctrine of transmigration of souls, or metempsychosis.

57. In which country did Kabbalism flourish most at the end of the third period?

In Spain, although nothing new was added.

58. Where else?

In Italy to some extent where, for instance, at the beginning of the 14th century Menachem from Rekanate wrote his famous Kabbalistic commentaries on the *Five Books of Moses* which totally correspond to the *Zohar*.

59. For what reason is the fourth period of Kabbalism in the 16th century distinguished?

Firstly, the fact that, as a result of the expulsion of Jews from Spain (1492) and the resulting migration of numerous Kabbalists, the interest in the Kabbala became more generally spread, especially in Palestine and Poland, as well as in Italy and elsewhere.[8] Secondly, the fact that during this time the systematic presentation of Kabbalistic speculation as well as the adaptation of letter mysticism with ascetical-ethical and magical tendencies reached its peak. Thirdly, the fact that only from this time on the Kabbalistic teachings became known to a great number of Christian scholars upon whose contemplations it had considerable influence.

60. Who was the main representative of the systematic speculative direction of Kabbalism during this period?
Mose (ben Jacob) Kordovero (1522-1570), a pupil of the famous Joseph Karo from Safed in Palestine, who is mainly known as the author of the Jewish ritual codex *Schulchan Aruch*.

61. What is Kordovero's main work called?
Pardes Rimmonim (Paradise of Pomegranates, see song 4 verse 3). He also wrote many other texts.

62. What new doctrine did he introduce?
The teaching of the Tzim'Tzum (see question 98).

Figure 4. Rabbi Isaac Lurja.

---

[8]Besides this fact, Kabbalistic writings were spread even further than before through the development of printing. Kabbalism remained only a secret doctrine insofar as it remained difficult to most because of its Hebrew (or Aramaic) language and the obsurity of its expression.

63. Who is the main representative of the ascetic-phonetic direction?

Isaac Lurja (1534-1572), idolized by his previous and later followers and also called "the lion" (Arî, meaning Adonênu Rabbi Jizchak, our lord Rabbi Isaac) or Rîha-Kâdôsch (St. Isaac). See Figure 4.

64. What were his fundamental thoughts?

That by way of extremely powerful attention ("Kewanah"), intention, and thinking (concentration) during the practice of religious rituals, through constantly absorbing oneself in the Zohar, by attentively reciting certain Kabbalistic formulas, by prayers in connection with losing oneself in meditation, and also by pious penetential exercise, one can reach a supernatural consciousness, soul, and perfection and, consequently, can cooperate with the salvation of the world.

65. Which teaching did he favor?

The teaching of transmigration of souls which he further developed in a curious way.

66. Did he leave us any writings?

No. To the contrary, he states that when he seriously concentrated on something the sources of supernatural wisdom were so powerfully open to him that he completely lacked the capability to write, and that he was hardly able to speak in order to communicate some of his revelations to his pupils.

67. How do his teachings come to us?

Mainly because of the notes of his best pupil Chajjim Vidal (ben Jozef Calabrese) who lived from 1543 to 1620, and who set down in his own writings, especially in the Ez chajjim (Tree of Life), much of what he had learned during his short apprenticeship in the last year of Lurja's life (1571-1572).

68. What are some examples of the great respect in which Lurja was held?

It was said that he visited the "heavenly academy" every night and that he received revelations of the highest wisdom there; his soul was believed to be a "spark of Moses' spirit" (see question 159). In fact it was even said that he was the "Messiah, the son of Joseph," meaning the predecessor of the actual Messiah (the son of David), though he did not reveal that out of modesty. Many miracles were also ascribed to him.

69. How does a modern Jewish scholar judge the influence of Lurja and Vidal?

Bloch says: Isaac Lurja and Chajjim Vidal are the cause of the fact that mystical, fanatical, and superstitious representations and very special and ascetic rituals influenced the life of Judaism as a whole. They assert that the *Zohar* was worshipped in a way that reminds one of idolatry, and that a vast prolific literature was developed that mixed together the *Zohar*, the *Bible*, and the *Talmud*, resulting in the most deformed fancies.

70. Mention some followers of the (speculative) direction of Moses Kordovero.

Samuel Gallico, his pupil, the author of *Assis Rimmon* (Pomegranate Juice, see song 8 verse 2)—Asarja de Fano (begins 17th century), author of *Asarah Maamroth* (The Ten Words) and *Pelach ha-Rimmon* (Piece of Pomegranate, see song 4 verse 3)—Nathan ben Salomo Spiro (who died in 1633), author of *Megalleh Amukkoth* (Discovery of Deep Things, see Job 12 verse 22)—Scheftel Horwitz (early 17th century), author of *Schefaltal* (Fullness of the Dew).

Figure 5. Sabbathai Zewi.

71. Mention some followers of Lurja's teachings.

Besides his pupil Chajjim Vidal (see question 67), Abraham de Herrera for instance (who died in 1639), author of *Schàar ha-Schamajim* or The Gate of Heaven, see *First Book of Moses* (Chapter 28, verse 17)— Napthali (ben Jacob) El-Hanan (middle 17th century author of the miraculous *Emek ha-Melech* or The King's-Veil (see *First Book of Moses,* Chapter 14 verse 17)—Jesaja Horwitz (see question 72)—and, finally, the famous and notorious Sabbathai Zewi (about 1666).

72. Which author of this group advocated the ethical direction?

Jesaja Horwitz (1517), author of the famous book *Schnê luchôth ha-berîth* (The Two Tables of the Covenant, see *Fifth Book of Moses,* Chapter 9, verse 9).

73. With whom did the fanatical direction reach its peak?

With the pseudo-messiah Sabbathai Zewi, a Kabbalist from Smirna, with whom almost all of Judaism fell in. Even after he converted to Islam in 1666 in Adrianopolis (out of fear of being killed by the Turkish government), the fanaticism he called into existence did not come to an end, but was propagated all over Europe by enthusiastic missionaries. It was still a spiritual power in the 18th century.

74. Who were the most important opponents of Sabbathairians?

The Amsterdam rabbi Zebi Hirsch Aschkenasi (1656-1718), who was driven out of his function by them, and his famous son Rabbi Altona (near Hamburg) Jacob Hirschel Emden (1696-1776), to whom Talmudism owes its victory over Sabbathairian heresy.

75. Which famous rabbi from those days was suspected of Sabbathairian tendencies?

The very assuming Talmudist and preacher Rabbi Jonathan Eibeschütz (1690-1764), rightly honored in modern science, who consequently brought upon himself the severe embitterment of Jacob Emden.

76. Why was Sabbathairianism considered heretical?

Because of the fact that it remodeled the teaching of the *Zohar* concerning the activity of the three principles, "Father, mother, and son" (see question 52) into a trinity and messianiac doctrine which corresponded largely to similar Christian views wherein the Godhead was considered a triad being, "the father was embodied within the son" (namely Sabbathai) encompassing the divine "Schechinah" (the Holy Spirit).

77. To what extent did Sabbathairianism mean the end of speculative Kabbalism?

The more the latter moved in the direction of Sabbathairianism the more it reached a path leading forward to the converted Christian teachers, and leading backward to the sharpened swords of its Talmudic opponents. The only ways out were: to the left, the path of profane philosophy that could only be set foot upon after laying down the shield of faith and the turban of fanaticism; to the right, the absorbing into magical superstitions for which one firstly had to extinguish the torch of speculation and throw away the sword of dialectics.

78. What made the Christian theologists and philosophers, especially in the beginning of this period, interested in the Kabbala?

The theologists believed to have found proof in it that Judaism, in spite of its resistance to the Christian religion, was in a roundabout way led by the Holy Spirit according to the basic principle of Christian dogma; so that, by its highly praised secret doctrines in particular, and even in spite of them, the truth of Christianity was proven. The followers of Plato, being the naturalistic philosophers of that time, saw in the Kabbala a welcome combination of theosophical-metaphysical and naturalistic monism and believed they had found the path leading to a solution of the world's mystery.

79. Mention a few of the Christian Kabbalists.

Johannes Pico van Mirandola (1463-1494), Johannes Reuchlin (1455-1522), and also Agrippa van Nettesheim (1487-1535) with whom

Johannes Pistorius and Christiaan Knorr of Rosenroth (author of the song, "Aurora of Eternity," who died in 1669), as translator and compiler of Kabbalistic writings, united.

80. Which writings of these men are especially remarkable?

Reuchlin's writings, *De verbo Mirifico* (1494) and *De arte Cabbalistica* (Hagenau 1513), Pistorius collection,[9] *Artis Cabbalisticae Scriptores* (Basel 1587), and Knorr of Rosenroth's *Kaballah denudata seu doctrina Ebraeorum transcendentalis et metaphysica atque theologica* (2 volumes, Sulzbach 1677 and Frankfurt 1684) [volume 2 contains translations from the *Zohar*]. Reuchlin started a sensation and studied Hebrew (with Leone da Modena) through getting to know the Kabbala while Rosenroth had, at his own cost, an edition of the *Zohar* published (Salzbach 1684).

81. Who were some of the philosophers influenced by the Kabbalistic teachings?

The naturalistic philosophers Theophrastus Paracelsus (1493-1541), Johan Baptist van Helmont (1577-1644), and his son Frans Mecurius van Helmont, together with the "Philosophus teutonicus," theosophist, and shoemaker Jacob Böhme from Görlitz (1575-1624); (see question 43).

82. Did the Kabbala have any influence on the philosophical system of Spinoza?

Isaac Misses and others have stated so but the similarity lies almost exclusively in the monistic doctrine of both systems and in the ethical principles of speculation (see question 118). The true teachings of Spinoza, like his negation of free will, are foreign, and even conflicting to the Kabbala (see question 132). More probable is the influence of the Kabbala on Cartesius and his school, especially on Professor Arnold Geulincx from Leiden from the same country and

---

[9]This contained, among other things, a translation of the book *Yetsirah* by Ricius, personal physician of Emperor Maximilian, who also became known as translator of sections of the *Talmud*. A better translation is the Latin one by Professor Stephan Rittangel (Konigsberg, 1642).

time of Spinoza, and who often literally copied him. As for the form, the Kabbala with its fantastic, glowing, colorful expressions, and its often confusing and mysterious representations is diametrically opposed to the mathematically clear, ice-cold, and plain expostulations of Spinoza.

83. What can be said about the last stage of Kabbalism?

After the Kabbala entered the stage described in question 77, which in some ways reminds one of Faust, and did not find its goal fulfilled, it dedicated itself, like Goethe's desperate thinker, completely to magic and fled into the dark corner of Hassidism, a confined Jewish ultra orthodoxy full of miracles and superstitions, which entered from Poland about the middle of the 18th century.

84. Do Kabbalists still exist?

Yes. Mostly in the semi-Asiatic countries like Poland, Russia, the Middle-East, etc.; they are the so-called wonder rabbis and their followers, who present themselves as representatives of a more or less strong superstition.

85. Do the Kabbalists teach a superstitious view of non-Jewish blood for some mystical purpose?

That is alleged but has not been proven. The example of the candidate Rabbi Bernstein from Breslow, who thought he could purify himself through some drops of blood from a Christian boy, was by all "insiders" considered a subjective religious mania.

86. Didn't the books of Aäron Briman demonstrate by two Kabbalistic writings that the shedding of non-Jewish blood in certain ceremonies was a God-pleasing sacrifice?

Those writings cited by Professor Rohling run very different in the original. They existed only in the translation with which Aäron Briman, a baptized Jew, misled the publisher from Padenborg as well as Professor Rohling from Prague.

87. But isn't this also stated in the Book *Gan naûl* (The Enclosed Garden) of Rabbi Mendel from Kossow?

Rabbi Mendel Hager from Kossow (Austria), who died around 1880 and whom Rohling referred to, has neither written such a work nor one with a similar title. Except for the linguistic work *Gan naûl* of Naphtali Hersch Wessely (Wesel 1725-1805), the experts in the trial Rohling-Bloch have found no book *Gan naûl* by Rabbi Mendel to quote.

88. Aren't there other books titled *Gan naûl?*

Certainly. One is *Gan naûl biûr debarim elahijjim be-ikrê haemunah* (Enclosed Garden, Statement on Divine Words about the Fundamental Principles of Religion), Amsterdam, 1629. Another is *Gan naûl al choljê ha-naschim u-mahûth bethulah we-ha-bethulim u-mikrêhem* (Enclosed Garden, Of Diseases of the Woman, Of the Nature of the Virgin, and Of Virginity and Its Characteristics), Venice, 1707, Jessnitz, 1721.

89. Do these books contain writings about blood?

The second book does, of course, though they speak exclusively about menstrual and virginal blood.

90. Is it possible that there exists a Kabbalistic manuscript under the name *Gan naûl?*

Indeed, among the Hebrew manuscripts of the Royal Library in Munich exists an unpublished manuscript of the Kabbalist Abraham Abulafia (see questions 30 and 34) titled *Gan naûl,* also called *Ozar éden ganûs* (The Hidden Treasure of Eden). It comprises a commentary on the book *Yetsirah* (see question 17) with highly confusing contents but no such thing as superstitious blood shedding.

91. Nevertheless, might such a blood superstition exist in some Jewish community in the world?

Why not, considering the fact that a scholar like Professor Strack has recorded so much about the blood superstition. Probabilities are not facts, however, and a superstition like that has nothing to do with either Kabbalism as far as it is an exclusively religious philosophy or with Judaism as recognized by the state.

92. Why will present-day Judaism have nothing more to do with Kabbalism?

Read *Aurora* by Jacob Böhme or another similar theosophical naturalistic work from the 16th century and then ask yourself whether you, as a modern person, could identify with the religious-ethical, the scientific, or even the artistic contents of the Kabbala—that is the answer!

CHAPTER 3

DOCTRINES OF THE KABBALA

93. Can one, in spite of the variety of the individual periods of development, directions, and contemplations, still speak of the doctrines of Kabbalism?
At least equally as much as a biblical doctrine of immortality, faith, salvation, etc., or a Talmudic ethic and so forth are spoken of. The Kabbala is in a relatively strong position since the *Zohar* is found to be a culmination point and a focus of the actual Kabbalistic doctrines, whereas the *Pardes Rimmonium* at the same time has systematized this material so that additional or deviating doctrines only have to be added.

94. Into which sections can the teachings of Kabbalism be divided?
1. Metaphysics of the Kabbalah: the doctrines of the absolute and its emanations.
2. Anthropology of the Kabbalah: psychology and ethics.
3. Magic of the Kabbalah: letter mysticism and practical Kabbalah.
First Division: Metaphysics.

95. What is the Godhead?

The highest comprehensible, the pure being, or the absolute. Within the pure conception of the highest is contained the idea that there can only be one being. This pure being must furthermore, in contrast to the imaginable and perceptible, be singular in every respect, neither complex nor changeable. As opposed to perishable things, the absolute (or the Godhead) is infinite, meaning outside space and time; unconditional, meaning caused or confined by nothing but itself, therefore inconceivable. All of this is comprised in the expression Èn sôph (the infinite, the unconditioned, the absolute).

96. Out of what follows that this absolute is not merely a product of thought but something actually existing?

It follows from the fact that the highest thinkable must be in all respects without shortcomings, because otherwise it would not be the highest imaginable. If it depended on matter, it would have imperfections and therefore not be the highest.

97. Isn't this conception of the Godhead totally pantheistical?

In the actual sense of the word, no more than the conception of the Godhead by the Neoplatonists. The One is not at the same time All, meaning "all things," but it exists for all other things and, in spite of the fact that these have their basis and origin in this One, it still remains the One, indivisible and unchangeable.

98. How is it possible that other beings outside the absolute that contains all true existence still have an individual existence?

Moses Kordovero tried to explain this by the teaching of the Tzim'Tzum (see question 60).

99. What is Tzim'Tzum?

It is usually translated as self-concentration or self-limitation (of the Godhead in favor of the world through which room for other beings originated). The Kabbalists warn, however, not to think of true expansion in this case and consider this process much more as supernatural.

100. What then should be understood by this term?

A self-modification of the Godhead, meaning that the one indivisible, unchangeable Godhead has reflected itself within itself as multiplicity without being absorbed within that multiplicity, just like the sun remains the same even though shining in numerous rays.

101. Why don't the Kabbalists such as Spinoza, for instance, say that this self-modification of the absolute only exists within our minds which can only imagine the limited, instead of ascribing this fact to the absolute?

Because otherwise the perishable substances, the independent modifications of the absolute, might be considered merely as a product of thinking, as sheer appearance.

102. Who dialectically showed the necessity of a self-modification of the absolute (without the name Tzim'Tzum)?

Asriêl ben Menachem (see question 30), who called this: "the power of the infinite over the limited." He says, "The infinite is perfect without fault. Saying that the infinite has (unlimited) power except on the limited would be equal to ascribing a shortcoming to perfection."

103. Is this world of things the result of the self-modification of the absolute?

Certainly not the direct result. For out of the infinite individual one and unchangeable, nothing that limited which is harmonic, various, and perishable as this material world could come forth.

104. How does Asriêl say this?

He writes: "Whoever would say that this perishable, limited, material world was the main thing originating from the infinite would at the same time ascribe the infinite a shortcoming since this world is far from perfect."

105. How does the Kabbala explain the transition of the infinite to the perishable condition?

It teaches that the infinite originally radiated reflections which, although not as clearly spiritual and complete as the infinite itself, were still very close to it. These are the Sephiroth (see question 26) or creative primeval thoughts. From these, other forces beamed forth which were less perfect and out of these, forces of still lower grade, and so on down through to the elements of the material world.

106. According to the Kabbala is the material world nothing but a lack of pure being—weakened primeval energy?

Exactly. The Kabbalistic emanation doctrine is philosophical energetics, metaphysical dynamics, wherein the Godhead or the absolute is the purest being as well as the highest energy (actus purus).

107. How does Asriêl (see question 102) express this?

He writes: "The limited primarily originated from the infinite (unlimited absolute) of the primeval thoughts (Sephiroth), which contain both the power of perfection as well as the power of imperfection. Namely, when the Sephiroth receive the abundance that flows from the perfection of the absolute, they are perfect power. However, lacking this their power is imperfect. Consequently, they possess the quality to work in a perfect as well as in an imperfect way. Perfection and imperfection are only the difference between different things."

108. Why are the Sephiroth simultaneously the highest regulating powers?

Since their energy (power output) shows three degrees of strength (highest, middle, and lowest degree), their emanations group accordingly in sequence. We usually imagine the image as a descending staircase. The Kabbalist prefers to see this fact as a decreasing alienation of the central primeval energy. Consequently any less perfect emanation is to him the cover or shell (Kelippah) of the preceding, and so the last (furthest) emanations being the so-called material things are the shell of the total and are therefore called (in the actual sense) Kelippoth.

109. How is the number 10 of the Sephiroth dialectically proven?

Since everything is the emanation of a corresponding higher power, one can conclude the number of primeval energies, or Sephiroth, from the number of elementary forces which rule the material world. Every force has three degrees (see question 108) of energy strength (highest, middle, and lowest) and also three dimensions (height, width, length), a total therefore of 9 with gravity as the tenth. From these ten material forces one can conclude ten primeval forces.

110. Of what does this deduction remind one?

Kant's effort to conclude from the number 12 and the conditions of judgement, the categories of pure reason.

111. What is the nature and the mutual relation of the ten Sephiroth?

Since the whole world is a force emanation of the Godhead, the Sephiroth, being the most direct primeval thoughts, are, as shown in their name, the spiritual, ethical forces (see question 119). They are divided into three groups of three Sephiroth, whereas the 10th Sephiroth represents the transition to the following lower world or stage of emanation. Within each of these three groups exists a positive (thesis, in the *Zohar*: masculine), a negative (antithesis, in the *Zohar*: feminine) and a mediating (synthesis, in the *Zohar*: son) principle. For the sake of clarity, the Sephiroth diagram is usually made up with all masculine principles at the right, all feminine at the left, and all mediating in the middle. In this way three linear series or pillars originate and the total represents the tree law, the Kabbalistic tree (*Arbor Kabbalistica*), the top of which is the highest (first) Sephirah and the root the 10th Sephirah.[10]

---

[10]The comparison to a tree is curious since the emanation goes from the top downward and this tree consequently rose from the top toward the roots. But whereas the ethical tendency of Kabbalistic thinking is based upon a development from imperfection toward perfection, the comparison is in that sense striking. As the metaphysical process goes from the top downward, the ethical striving goes from the bottom upward.

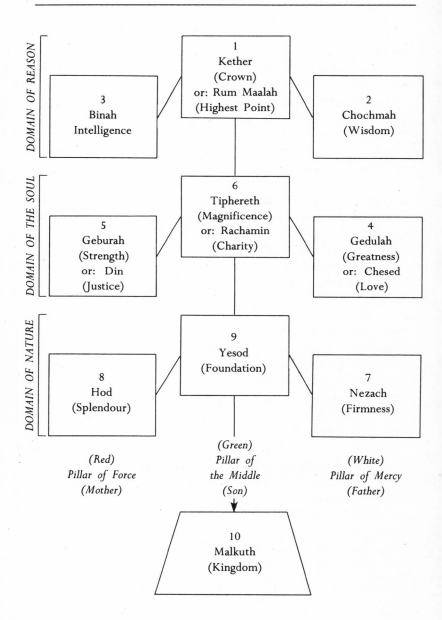

Figure 6. The 10 Sephiroth on the Kabbalistic Tree.

112. How are the divisions of the 10 Sephiroth classified with the *Arbor Kabbalistica?*
Figure 6 is the simple schematical representation. Many others exist in addition to this; for example, the Sephiroth as emanations of the absolute (Figure 7 on page 34), or as members of the metaphysical primeval man (Adam Kadmoni), as seen in Figure 9 on page 42, and in question 149.

113. How is the totality of the Sephiroth described?
As the world of the (first) emanation (Azilah Aziluth), the highest of the total of the four worlds (emanation stages) of the universe for which the other names are adopted from *Isaiah* (Chapter 43 verse 7).

114. What are the other three worlds called?
Underneath the Azilah world comes the 2, the world of creation (Beriah), under that 3, the world of formation (Yetsirah), under that 4, the world of making (Asijjih) (see question 124).

115. How are these worlds organized?
They are totally analogous to the world of the Sephiroth (Azilah), divided in 10 divisions or subspheres corresponding to the Sephiroth which, however, are spiritual, and at the same time formed after a similar fashion differing only insofar that each following lower world is less spiritually pure and of a more coarse nature than the one before so that it is the shell (Kelippah) of the latter.

116.[11] Is the lowest (Asijjah) world the physical world?
Yes, but Asijjah also contains spiritual elements, although on the lowest stage and in very obscure form. Matter is to Kabbalism not something individual or original (see question 106) but an *öv*, a lack of pure spiritual being—just like darkness is a lack of light. Just as the Kabbala does not know absolute dualism (fundamental difference) between spirit and matter but is, to the contrary, monistic, even the material elements (the Kelippoth in the true sense—question 108)

---

[11]Questions 116 through 120 can be avoided by beginners in this philosophical inquiry.

Figure 7. Star-shaped representation of the Sephiroth.

cannot, according to its doctrines, be exclusively dead matter. Everything is but an emanation of primeval unity, of pure spirit. Therefore everything is animated, although in differing degrees.

117. The material elements and apparitions (Kelippoth) are, however, used (mainly with the Sephiroth) as the polarity of the spiritual elements.

Certainly, but in the same way that impure and pure, troubled and clear, imperfect and perfect, unconscious and conscious, etc. are contrasted. Were the polarity absolute then the development from this lowest level upward to the pure—the perfect whereon the Kabbala is based—could not take place. Throughout the metaphysics of the Kabbala runs an ethical fundamental line, namely that even the lowest elements are still emanations of the primeval unity. However weak they may be, they are still the spirit of spirits.

118. Of which philosopher is one reminded?
Spinoza, who called his main work *Ethica*. Although this work deals mainly with metaphysics and rational anthropology—and especially the theory of understanding and emotions—and deals little with ethics as a rational doctrine of virtue, the fundamental conception and the goal of the total work is of an ethical nature.

119. Can the combination of metaphysics and ethics in the complexity of the Sephiroth doctrines be pointed out more specifically?
Yes, first the three highest Sephiroth represent the domain of reason as reason is closest to the absolute and, therefore, its first emanation (see question 112). Since the world must be imagined as an organism, its highest principle which develops and regulates everything is reason. Theoretical reason or wisdom (Chochmah) which orders the thoughts by way of thinking, containing the world as a thought, is opposed to practical reason or intelligence (Binah) which assimilates thoughts representing the world as manifested willpower. Both, however, unite in the highest reason (Rûm màalah) which includes all rational force and all thoughts originating from intuition.[12]

Second, a continuation of the domain of thinking and wanting is the domain of feeling and perception, the domain of the soul (see question 112). Observed are quantity and quality having their highest confluence in proportion. Metaphysically worded, this is the union of greatness (Gedulah) and strength (Geburah) in the magnificence of the beautiful proportion (Tiphèreth). Ethically conceived it is the union of the wholehearted comprehensive love (Chèsed) and the intensive stern justice (Din) in charity (Rachamim), which has as attributes the comprehensive feeling of affection as well as the powerful feeling of righteousness.

Third, from the domain of perception flows the domain of nature, meaning the principles of the visible world. Here firmness (Nèzach),

---

[12]Some Kabbalists place Kether (or Rûmàalah) above all Sephiroth and assume Dàath (reason, thinking) as the mediating principle between Chochmah and Binah without, however, counting it since they consider Dàath more a reflection of the Sephiroth Kether.

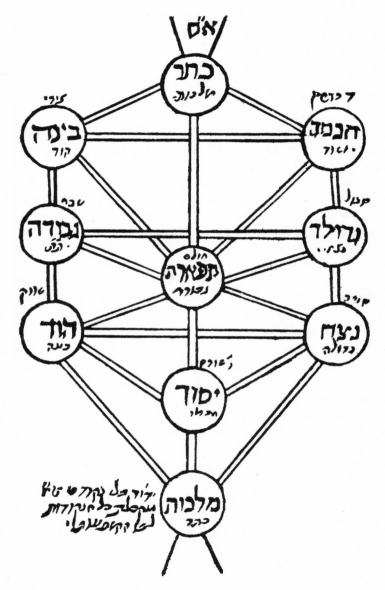

Figure 8. Kabbalistic tree from a *Zohar* manuscript.

meaning the ability to persevere of the material principle, and splendor (Hôd), meaning the ability to develop of the force principle, find their highest confluence in the foundation (Jesôd), meaning substance.

120. Why is it that the calm principles (Chochmah, Chèsed, Nèzach), or the pillars of mercy (see question 112), are denoted as masculine and the active manifesting (Binah, Din, Hôd), or the pillars of force, as feminine?

The latter are rightly imagined as originating from the former, like Eve came forth from Adam's rib; activity originates from rest, will from thought, intensity from extensity, force from matter. Since these second principles (Binah, etc.) not only originate from the first (Chochmah, etc.) but also primarily receive substance and activity from them, they are in this connection receptive, like the woman is in connection with man, and are therefore (in spite of the name "pillars of force") feminine in nature. The nature of the woman (especially in eastern and southern countries) is more mutable and more intense than that of the man.

121. Why is the mediating principle also called "son" in spite of the fact that it stands above the other two, that it contains them as attributes, and that it is not only represented as their higher combination but also as their origin?

The conception "son" (child) logically raises the conceptions "father" and "mother" just as the principle "middle pillar" logically raises those of the two other "pillars" (see questions 111 and 112). Normally, the "son" also physically unites the individual characteristics of the father and the mother. Finally, a "son" (child) is in the ethical sense the most logical connection between the parents.

122. What is the meaning of the 10 Sephirah "Kingdom" (Malkuth)?

In a sense these Sephirah represent the borderland, the gateway to the nearest lower world, Beriah (see question 114). Also the word Altèreth (garland), which the Sephirah are often called, includes the conception of binding and connecting as well as the indication of the lower place of the Sephirah as opposed to the highest (Kèther, crown). Just as the garland as headdress belongs to the realm of the crown but takes a lower position, the 10 Sephirah belong to the highest emanations but are the lowest of them.

123. What can be said regarding the above-mentioned (see question 109) comparison of the 10 Sephirah to gravity?
Just as gravity strives downward and pulls the other forces down, the 10 Sephirah in the same way are the transition to the lower emanations.

124. What does the *Beriah* world contain? (See question 114.)
The 10 primeval forms or concepts of creation. In Platonism and Neoplatonism these concepts are represented as spiritual intelligent beings.

125. What does the next highest world, *Yetsirah*, contain?
The heavenly spheres as well as the angels and souls (compare the doctrine of the soul in the second section).

126. What does the lowest world, *Asijjah*, contain?
This is the world of material apparitions in the Kabbalistic sense (see question 116).

127. How are the four worlds of the descending emanation related?
They are mutually, as a whole and its parts, in close connection and in exchange of spiritual nature. Therefore, spiritual elevation from the lowest levels of existence to the higher regions is possible and man, out of the circle of material things that surround him, can be initiated into spiritual spheres.

CHAPTER 4

ANTHROPOLOGY OF THE KABBALA

128. Are the psychological and ethical doctrines of the Kabbala distinctly separated?

No. They are rather closely connected and although the psychological doctrines have no goal within themselves, they are almost completely subservient to mysticism.

129. In what way are the psychological doctrines of the Kabbala connected with the Sephiroth doctrines?

The three parts or active principles of the soul—neschamah, the soul gifted with reason; rûach, the experiencing soul; nèphesch, the vegetative soul or the soul as a living part of the body—correspond to the three main groups of Sephiroth—the domain of reason, that of the soul, and that of nature (see question 112)—and they directly originate from the Sephiroth and are under their influence. The descending influence of the 10th Sephirah (see questions 109 and 122) can immediately become activated when the soul, under certain circumstances, descends to a lower level of existence than the one it held up until then.

130. Does the soul consist of three parts?

No. In the same way that the Sephiroth (in spite of its tenfoldedness) or the Sephiroth domain (in spite of its threefoldedness) represent a self-contained world organism, the soul, in spite of its so-called "parts," is a self-contained organic whole.

131. What is the ethical meaning of the doctrine which states that the souls desend from Sephiroth and are under their influence?

It explains the possibility that the soul can, under certain circumstances and by certain deeds, free itself of its material limits and imperfections and can elevate itself into higher spiritual spheres (see questions 117 and 127).

132. Does the Kabbala therefore teach a moral freedom of the soul?

Yes, as opposed to the other monistic systems like those of Spinoza, for example (see question 82). This is a very important point.

133. Doesn't this contradict the fundamental thought that all emanation processes of the absolute, therefore the existence and the freedom of souls included, are based on a metaphysical causality?

Kabbalism does not recognize this contradiction. It does not even mention it. From an ethical point of view the soul, through its descent from a higher world, has an essential urge toward its origin, a natural desire for perfection, and an innate tendency toward good which can indeed be liable to weakness but which will nevertheless persevere and attain its goal.

134. How can this be proven?

According to the teachings of the Kabbalists all souls become blessed, meaning that they all return to the higher regions from which they originate. A similar doctrine is the one of Father Origenes.

135. How can the nonstriving of the soul upward be considered a sin?

Because of the possibility, the ability to strive upward implies an obligation to do so. Since its character is energy (see question 106) the soul is destined to overcome all obstacles. Since the possibility of doing this is within its power, it is its own fault if it does not act accordingly.

136. Can the soul be called created in the actual sense?

No. It is an emanation of the living primeval forces of Sephiroth and by way of these, it is an extended though low emanation of the absolute.

137. When did the soul come into being?

As an emanation of the absolute it might have eternally existed within and have had, therefore, an ideal pre-existence since, according to the doctrine of the Kabbalists, all souls were created at the same time. Consequently, on the one hand the soul is eternal and on the other it had a beginning before any physical existence.

138. Where was the soul before it reached a physical state?

In connection with the Talmudic contemplations on pre-existence the Kabbalists teach that it was in the Yetsirah domain (see question 125), specifically in a part of the spheres of the heavens *Araboth,* called *Gûph.*

139. According to this doctrine, have all souls entered the physical earthy existence?

No, some souls are still waiting.

140. What has become of the souls that have come to earth?

They are to be partially found in the first earthy existence, though for the greater part they undergo the transmigrations of the soul through different succeeding earthy periods of existence. Some souls have already elevated to a higher life.

141. Where do these elevated souls go to?

There are different opinions on this matter. According to the most rational views, the final goal of the perfect soul is detachment in the absolute, the "ocean of the Godhead" (see question 116).

142. What is the nature of the soul in its pre-existential existence?

Male-female, meaning asexual. (The body of the first man was imagined in the same way by Plato as well as in the *Talmud* and *Midrasch*.)

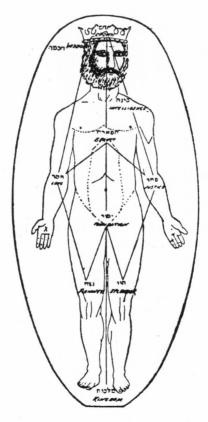

Figure 9. The Sephiroth as the total of man (see 112 and 146).

143. In what state do the pre-existential souls find themselves?

In a conscious state. They have knowledge of their thoughts (see questions 124 and 146) so that, according to Plato as well, all mundane science is but a retrospective recollection of this pre-existential knowledge.

144. For what purpose do souls enter this physical earthly existence?

For perfection!

145. Thus not as punishment, as is taught by Plato and others?

No. This is neither a Jewish nor an original Kabbalistic view. To the contrary, the souls enter the body pure and free of sin so that they can remain pure and become more perfect in the struggle against the sensual and material on earth. This must be accomplished through their own force.

146. Is it not taught, however, that the souls sinned in pre-existential existence and therefore had to enter bodies?

Yes and no. The school of Lurja (see question 63) in particular advocates that originally all souls were united in the pre-existence of the first human beings, meaning in the idea of man, and have therefore sinned at the same time as the first man. Thus, they did not enter the world as a direct punishment but more for the sake of purification after they had previously been clothed with the ideal physical form in the domain Beriah (see questions 114 and 124).

147. What can be conjectured about these sins of pre-existence?

The Indian, Greek, and Christian doctrines of a pre-existence, which all assume a fall of the soul during that pre-existence resulting from an unlawful desire for the material and therefore causing the incarnation of these souls, have undoubtedly influenced the representation of the sinning of all souls in the first Adam. The doctrine of original sin by the Apostle Paul appears to have especially contributed to this, although Lurja didn't recognize this doctrine as Christian.

148. Is this sin in the actual sense?

Certainly no individual sin of the soul, since it had no independent existence when it sinned in Adam and was therefore not free to choose and act. Consequently we are not speaking of a culpable deed but of a metaphysical expression for the devaluation which a soul experiences out of necessity when it enters the material world. Since this is, however, a necessary process there can be no sin or punishment. Kabbalism and the entire Jewish teachings point out that only when there has actually been sin can there be punishment.[13]

149. Then human souls are not burdened by sin?

They are. This sin, however, is a result of the earthly material existence and actually not so much a deed as a dereliction of duty, namely a complete or partial neglect to strive upward to spiritual and moral perfection. As in almost every monism, sin is thus basically negative, a privation. It is a culpable dereliction of duty, a negative state of will, opposed to the objective striving of the soul (see question 133) to the higher and the good. Depending on the degree of moral strength of the will, all human beings are more or less sinful.

150. How can souls, in spite of this condition of sin, reach moral perfection?

By remaining in the earthly existence until they have conquered their material shortcomings and finally return, as victors, from the struggle against imperfection.

151. How is this attained?

By metempsychosis (Gilgul, see question 56).

152. Where does the belief in the transmigration of souls originate?

In Indian Brahmanism. From there it penetrated to the Egyptians and the Greeks. It played a special role in Platonism and Neoplatonism and appears to have reached Kabbalism by way of the latter.

---

[13]Not punishment for an unavoidable sin (fate), as in other doctrines of pre-existence.

153. How is the Kabbalistic transmigration of souls distinguished from that of the Greek?
In contradiction to the Greek, the Kabbala assumes a necessity for a plural metempsychosis for all human beings since one human lifetime is not sufficient to reach the necessary moral perfection as stated in the metempsychosis doctrine, especially in that of the Buddhistic.[14]

154. What distinguishes the Kabbalistic doctrine of transmigration of souls from that of the Buddhistic?
According to the Kabbala, the soul as a whole passes to the new existential form. According to Buddhism (which negates the substance of the soul), the personality (meaning the aggregate of certain qualities which the soul up to then possesses) perishes at death and passes only the main individuality of the soul, the will to live, to the new life to gain new qualities over and over again.

155. What forms does the soul return in after death?
In those corresponding to the spiritual and moral perfection it had reached at the time of death; in higher or lower organized human bodies, animal bodies (mammals, birds, fish, reptiles, insects, and mollusks),[15] or in plants and leaves, even in stones, clay, dust, water, or possibly in tools. Several Kabbalists do not extend metempsychosis any further than human or, at the most, higher animal bodies.

156. Can it also return in bodies of the opposite sex?
That is considered possible (see question 180) although it is usually assumed that the up until now male souls return in male bodies and female souls return in female bodies (in the same way it is considered Jewish souls sometimes can enter non-Jewish bodies and non-Jewish souls can return in Jewish bodies).

---

[14]See Olcott, *Buddhistic Catechism.* (page 48).
[15]According to some, the soul returns in these lower forms only if it has not perfected itself in the course of three human migrations.

157. Do transmigrating souls enter only embryonic bodies or also those of living adults?
Generally, one assumes the first but the other possibility, which the teachings of the *Ibbur* refers to, must also be considered.

158. Do transmigrating souls enter another body immediately after the death of the body they have lived in?
The prevailing opinion seems to be that the bodiless souls wander about the earth for a certain period of time until they find a body that corresponds with their present state or one that will correspond with it in the future.

159. Can a soul divide itself in order to enter several bodies simultaneously?
Yes. At least the opinion is held that a soul, for the salvation of mankind (especially the soul of a good and wise man), can divide itself into a number of sparks which then become the souls of eminent men. According to other views, these "spark-souls" are not fragments but dynamic radiations of perfect souls from great men.[16]

160. Is it also possible for two or more souls to exist within one body at the same time?
Another or even many other souls whose bodies have passed away can join the "resident" soul of a living body as a sort of sub-soul. They can thus, for a certain period, be more or less intimately connected with the main soul of the body. This is the so-called "Ibbur" or impregnation of souls.

161. When and for what purpose does "Ibbur" take place?
When a soul cannot sufficiently perfect itself in spite of its good will, or out of ignorance, then one or more wandering souls join it (after the death of their own bodies) to assist it. This gives the impression of a completely different spirit suddenly coming over someone. When the soul has gathered sufficient moral strength, these sub-souls can

---

[16]In the same way that the Sephiroth (see question 105) are not fragments but energy activities of the one unchangeable absolute.

withdraw without resulting in the person's death. In addition it is, at least according to Lurja's followers, also possible that one or more souls of unrepentant persons (evil-doers, etc.) after the death of their bodies may join the main soul of a man corresponding to their state. This is their own punishment in part but is also the torment of the now-possessed person with whom they stay until they are driven out through exorcism (see question 180).

162. What is the difference between Gilgul and Ibbur?
In the case of Gilgul, the soul destined for transmigration enters a new body wherein it stays until death, trying to fulfill the up to now unfulfilled duties of life. In the case of Ibbur, the transmigrating soul enters a body already having a main soul and unites only temporarily with this soul to either morally support or punish it.

163. Do most people have very old main or sub-souls?
Yes. This follows from the Kabbalistic line of thought that the number of created (emanated) human souls (see question 137) has been limited. (According to many, 60,000.) A descent of never-before incarnated souls out of the Gûph only takes place to replace the souls which, through gaining the highest perfection, were taken away from earth.

164. What is the basis of the Kabbalistic doctrine of transmigration of souls?
Other than unquestionable indications from a number of bible verses, it is mainly based on the following arguments (by Manasse ben Israel, 1604-1657): Punishment without guilt is not compatible with the conception of a world order which is based on divine goodness, justice, and compassion. Nevertheless we frequently see that good and righteous people are constantly suffering, whereas the wicked often enjoy undisturbed happiness, although it should in all equity be the other way around; that children, many from birth on, have the most terrible handicaps or are born as unfortunate misfits in apparent contradiction of the all goodness of the creator who can only bring forth the good; that children die very young before they could have sinned on earth which is in total contradiction to divine compassion. At the

same time young children without thinkable guilt are hit by all sorts of plagues and accidents.

Only the doctrines of transmigration and pre-existence solve these drawbacks in a logical and satisfying way and state that: Those now suffering expiate their guilt built up in a previous existence. Consequently, when they live virtuously they will be rewarded in a following existence. The now-fortunate evil-doers were good in a previous earthly existence; they now enjoy their reward while at the same time they create for themselves through their crimes a better fate in a next life. Those born deformed, handicapped, etc., are persons whose souls

Figure 10. Manasse ben Israel.

are deformed because they have heavily sinned in a previous existence, and for this reason they have entered in bodies as punishment. The souls of those dying young or of those punished in early childhood with accidents, etc., are also souls which in a previous existence have heavily sinned. Therefore as punishment, they are not allowed within the new body for long but are transmigrated to another one. For not only death (disembodiment) but also reincarnation is something unpleasant and difficult for the soul.

165. What happens to the souls that have finally reached perfection after many transmigrations?
All souls will reach this perfection (see question 134) and will, after the successfully fulfilled life struggle, return to their origin.

166. Where is this origin?
That is not quite clear. Several Kabbalists assume a personal continued existence of the purified souls in the world of Yetsirah, Beriah, or the Sephiroth in such a way that the individual parts of the soul return to different sections. Others teach a confluence of the souls, a flowing back of all emanations into the endless, the absolute, the Oceanus Divinitatis. Whether this course is another emanation process as taught by stoics (and others) is not mentioned, since in the ethical sense only the present emanation is considered.

CHAPTER 5

MAGIC OF THE KABBALA

167. What is Kabbalistic magic about?
The evoking of supernatural powers (wonders) by way of the holy
name of God and the different forms of it (letter compositions, etc.).

**168. Does the Kabbala contain black magic as well as white
magic?**
Yes, it also knows the evoking of demonic, meaning non-divine,
powers although it rejects that as witchcraft (Kischûph).

**169. What is the person called whose knowledge of God's
name is sufficiently great to perform miracles?**
Bàal schêm (Lord of the Name) or *Bàal schêm tôb* (Lord of the good
Name, in short, *Bescht*), whereas a magician is called *mekasch-schèph*.

**170. On what does one base the belief that miracles can be
performed with the name of God?**
The *Bible* already mentions the performance of miracles "in the name
of God" (Hebrew be-schem, by the name). Since the name of something must express the character of that thing, so also is God's name

the expression and revelation of its being. And since the being of the Godhead (see question 106) is absolute power (Almightiness), the use of its name must also be a seizure of its being, an absorption of its power (as far as this is possible). The individual letters of God's name are also parts of the being, the energy of the Godhead. Consequently the knowledge of different combinations, according to certain rules, gives the ability to raise a certain power to a certain purpose.

171. Are the names of the angels also used?
Yes, as well as other magical formulas. The angels are considered servants of God, meaning power outlets of the Godhead, and the magical formulas are being used "in the name" of the Godhead. This is in keeping with the use of the original formula, the name of God.

172. Which name of God is used for performing miracles?
Schèm ha-mephorasch, the spoken name.

173. Who was the first to use it?
Lilith, "Adam's first wife" (as she is called in Goethe's *Faust,* Part 2). The *Talmud* and the *Kabbala* believe that the woman mentioned in the *First Book of Moses* (verse 1) was an earlier wife of Adam than the

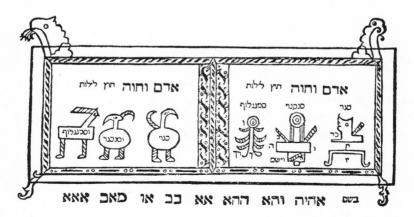

Figure 11. Amulet for assistance during a difficult delivery (see Question 174). On the left and the right are the names of the three angels.

woman mentioned in the *First Book of Moses* (verse 2) who came out of his rib. The first woman must have been of a very fierceful and ambitious nature who, out of her intercourse with Adam, produced demons. Lilith wanted to take the role of the man in their marriage, and when Adam forbade her she spoke God's name and fled. From then on, as mother of the demons, she did harm to all pregnant women and newly born children.

174. How was this abuse of God's name punished?

When Lilith fled to Egypt (the later mother country of witchcraft) God sent the three angels Senoi, Sansenoi, and Samangeloph after her. They were going to drown her since she refused to return to Adam; she saved her life by promising not to hurt pregnant women or children while they were guarded by the names of these three angels. Ever since that time, the three names of the angels (solemnly spoken as well as written on parchment in the maternity room) have been employed as an amulet for mother and child. (See Figure 11.)[17]

175. Whom else does the Kabbala ascribe miracles to performed with the use of God's name?

To Eliesar, the servant of Abraham who, when he found Rebecca at the well, had to prove his divine mission to Laban by pronouncing God's name and making all his camels rise in the air with himself elevated above them.

176. What is said about David in connection with miracles?

By speaking God's name, Abisai made him levitate thereby escaping his pursuers. While laying the foundation for the temple David is believed to have found the "Eben Schtijah" (stone of depth) which covers the "source of great depth" (*First Book of Moses,* Chapter 7 verse 11) and wherein the Schêm ha-mephorasch (see question 172) was inscribed. It further states that he brought this stone to the Holy of Holies where it served for the foundation of the Ark of the Covenant. Bold pupils of wise men now and then penetrated the sanctuary and

---

[17]See Figure 12 on page 54 for another example of an amulet for mother and child.

learned from the stone its "name" and its letter combinations by
which they performed miracles.

177. What other effects of the "Schêm" are mentioned?

The raising of the dead, the evoking of souls, the healing of the sick,
metamorphosis, exorcism, the killing and creating of living creatures,
walking on the water, the understanding of all languages, etc. In the
book *Rasiêl* (see question 22) it is stated: By the naming of the Schêm
one can exorcise devils, extinguish fires, cure diseases, and ban
thoughts; by pronouncing and writing it one can destroy an enemy and
inspire the love of a ruler. By means of this, Moses killed the Egyptians
(*Second Book of Moses*, Chapter 2 verse 12), etc.

Figure 12. Amulet for the protection of lying-in woman and the new-
born child.

178. What are some examples of raising the dead?

The raising of the widow's son in Sarepta by Elia was said to be done by means of the schêm. [A Jewish saga in the "Tholdoth Jeschu," etc., also ascribes the raising of the dead and other miracles performed by Jesus to the Schêm]. Rabbi Chanina bar Chama is believed to have brought the slave of the Roman emperor Antonius back to life and to have won the emperor over to Judaism that way. Antonius often secretly visited the patriarch Juda I (about 200 A.D.). For the purpose of keeping these visits secret he always had his accompanying slaves killed at the door of the Jewish scholar. When Rabbi Chanina, however, saw the dead while visiting his fellow-believer, he brought them back to life through the use of the Name to the great surprise of the emperor, who found his dead slaves alive again.

179. What are some examples of metamorphosis?

Once, a rabbi met a witch who tried to put a spell on him. He spoke the Name, changing her into a donkey which he cheerfully took to the market to sell.

180. And exorcisms?

Solomon had the entire world of spirits subjected to him by the Schêm (engraved upon his seal ring and chain) until the demon Asmodi pilfered the ring from him thus obtaining power himself. The expelled Solomon wandered about until he finally got the ring back from the stomach of a fish, whereafter he banned Asmodi. Also interesting is Lurja's story of the exorcism of a spirit who possessed a woman. The spirit was the soul of a drowned Jew who had no death bed and had done no penance. After long wanderings it was allowed to enter a woman when she was swearing and the epileptic-hysterical woman suffered terribly. Lurja talks and acts with her tormentor in the same way as the Christian exorcist; he calls it names and lets it tell its story. With the help of the "Name" he finally forces the spirit to withdraw into the little toe of the woman, which it does with the usual violence.

181. What are some examples of apparitions?

The high Rabbi Löw from Prague (Juda ben Bezalêl who died in 1600) supposedly had the patriarchs and sons of Jacob appear in front of Rudolf II by means of the power of the Schêm.

182. And some examples of creations?

The *Talmud* states that the Rabbis Chanina and Oschaja created a fattened calf for every sabbath, disposing of it in honor of the holy day. A famous rabbi (according to the same source) even created a human form and sent this to his friend, Rabbi Sira. Since the pseudo-man could not speak, however, Rabbi Sira knew it was of magical origin and had it returned to dust.

Older Judaism knows the story of the "Golem" of the high Rabbi Löw. The Golem, a sexless human shape, was formed out of a lump of mold. When the rabbi put a piece of parchment inscribed with the Schêm in its mouth, the lump came alive and fulfilled through the week all services ordered by its master. Friday evening, when the Sabbath started, Löw took the parchment out of its mouth and during the whole Sabbath the monster would just lie as a lifeless mass. At the end of Sabbath he would call it to life again by means of the Schem. One Friday evening the rabbi went to the synagogue without taking the Schêm out of the Golem's mouth. The monster not only continued working but gained such power through the strengthened activity of the Schêm on Sabbath that it soon started destroying everything, throwing over houses, etc. Scared and shocked, people sent for the master in the synagogue. Löw walked toward the furious creature, took the parchment out of its talking mouth, and it disintegrated. Löw is also believed to have evoked the entire Hradschin in Prague in his study in the presence of Emperor Rudolf.

183. What languages can be understood with the help of the Schêm?

All sounds and whisperings (meaning thoughts): the different human languages, the animal languages, the conversations of the angels and demons, the rustling of the trees, the murmuring of the sea, and the unspoken thoughts of fellow creatures. King Solomon much have been especially skillful in this respect with the help of the Schêm.

184. What particular caution should be taken with the use of the Schêm?

He who wants to perform some magical act must possess total physical purity, and the right grouping of the symbols and their correct pronunciation (a secret known but to very few) are essential. The one that speaks the formula in a state of impurity will die or at least risk his life, as will also he who becomes impure during the miraculous act.

185. Can the Schêm be employed only by men?

Generally speaking, yes. Other than Lilith, a girl named Ichtahar used the Schem to find refuge in heaven when the angel Schamchasu wanted to prostitute her. This is an individual case though, probably originating from Babylonian mythology.

186. For what purposes are amulets employed?

For inspiring love and killing enemies, but they are especially used for protection against demons and all sorts of calamities (see questions 16, 174, and 177).

187. Where does one find the first Jewish historical records regarding amulets?

Actually the *Thephillin* (Filateries) and the *Mezuzah* (cylinder-shaped amulets containing pieces of parchment inscribed with bible verses and fastened on door posts) are a form of the amulet from Talmudic rabbinistic Judaism. Their efficacy is based on the words within and the name of God.

188. What do the Kabbalistic amulets contain?

Various names of God and of the angels as well as formulas with blessings or curses and obscure and almost incomprehensible letter combinations.

189. What are some examples of these combinations?

The *Talmud* gives a prophylactic against eye diseases (in the treaty *Pesachim* 120A), the formula "Schebririn" which is written in such a way that the letters of the word evenly lessen whereby the disease does the same as shown in Figure 13.

More famous is the "Abracadabra" that wanders about in magic books and which was praised as a means against fever by the Roman Serenus Sammonicus. The formula is shown in Latin in Figure 14 and in Hebrew in Figure 15.

שכרירי
ברירי
רירי
ירי
רי

Figure 13. To lessen the disease.

Figure 14. The Abracadabra formula in Latin.

אבר, אכדברא
בר, אכדבר
ראכדב
אכד
כ

א ב ר כ ד א ר ב ר א
א ב ר כ ד א ב ר
א ב ר כ א ר ב
א ב ר א כ ר
א ב ר א כ
א ב ר א
א ב ר
א

Figure 15. The Abracadabra formula in Hebrew.

190. What does "Abracadabra" mean?

Abbara Kedabra means "Flee like these words"; it is said to the one who is sick.[18] All other explanations are, for the greater part, very unlikely (for instance Ab, ruach, dabar, meaning father, spirit, "word" or son) or more far-fetched than this (for instance Dr. Fischer's "Abed Kadabar," meaning "do as decided," a recipe formula for which, however, the letters need to be changed).

191. What do some of the other amulets contain?

Secret cipher combinations, the words of which sometimes have a peculiar, partially mysterious relation with the doctrines of the Sephiroth and others. An example of this is the seven-square (with the original in Hebrew ciphers) shown in Figure 16.

---

[18]With a slight alteration: Abbada Kedabra, meaning "decrease as this word (formula) decreases."

24	47	16	41	10	35	04
05	23	48	17	42	11	29
30	06	24	49	18	36	12
13	31	07	25	43	19	37
38	14	32	01	26	44	20
21	39	08	33	02	27	45
46	15	40	09	34	03	28

Original:

ד	לה	ר	מא	מז	מג	כב
כט	יא	מב	יז	נח	כג	ה
יב	לו	יח	טע	כד	ו	ל
לז	יט	מג	כה	ז	לא	יג
כ	מד	כו	א	לב	יד	לה
נח	כז	ב	לג	ח	לט	כא
כח	ג	לד	ט	מ	טו	מו

Figure 16. The 7 square.

The sum is always 175. Or look at the eight-square shown in Figure 17. Notice the lengthwise, transverse, and diagonal returning sum of 260. The nine-square has the sum of 369, as shown in Figure 18.

08	58	59	05	04	62	63	01
49	15	14	52	53	11	10	56
41	23	22	44	45	19	18	48
32	34	35	29	28	38	39	25
40	26	27	37	36	30	31	33
17	47	46	20	21	43	42	24
09	55	54	12	13	51	50	16
64	02	03	61	60	06	07	57

Figure 17. The 8 square.

37	78	29	70	21	62	13	54	05
06	38	79	30	71	22	63	14	46
47	07	39	80	31	72	23	55	15
16	48	08	40	81	32	64	24	56
57	17	49	09	41	73	33	65	25
26	58	18	50	01	42	74	34	66
67	27	59	10	51	02	43	75	35
36	68	19	60	11	52	03	44	76
77	28	69	20	61	12	53	04	45

Figure 18. The 9 square.

192. Are there also letter squares?

Yes, in great numbers and different combinations. Figure 19 contains a square of the word Elohim, or God.

Rosenroth (see question 79) gives a similar example of the verse "Ex uno centro sua mittit lumina Zohar" in a square of 31 times 31 letters. Long Bible proverbs are also written in a similar way as formulas for protection and blessing, as well as the earlier mentioned names of God and the angels, etc. Figure 20 shows an imitation in German.

ם	י	ה	י	ם
י	ה	ל	ה	י
ה	ל	א	ל	ה
י	ה	ל	הָ	י
ם	י	ה	י	ם

Figure 19. The Elohim square.

H	C	I	D	E	T	Ü	H	E	H	Ü	T	E	D	I	C	H
C	I	D	E	T	Ü	H	E	B	E	H	Ü	T	E	D	I	C
I	D	E	T	Ü	H	E	B	R	B	E	H	Ü	T	E	D	I
D	E	T	Ü	H	E	B	R	R	R	B	E	H	Ü	T	E	D
E	T	Ü	H	E	B	R	R	E	R	R	B	E	H	Ü	T	E
T	Ü	H	E	B	R	R	E	H	E	R	R	B	E	H	Ü	T
Ü	H	E	B	R	R	E	H	R	H	E	R	R	B	E	H	Ü
H	E	B	R	R	E	H	R	E	R	H	E	R	R	B	E	H
E	B	R	R	E	H	R	E	D	E	R	H	E	R	R	B	E
H	E	B	R	R	E	H	R	E	R	H	E	R	R	B	E	H
Ü	H	E	B	R	R	E	H	R	H	E	R	R	B	E	H	Ü
T	Ü	H	E	B	R	R	E	H	E	R	R	B	E	H	Ü	T
E	T	Ü	H	E	B	R	R	E	R	R	B	E	H	Ü	T	E
D	E	T	Ü	H	E	B	R	R	R	B	E	H	Ü	T	E	D
I	D	E	T	Ü	H	E	B	R	R	E	H	Ü	T	E	D	I
C	I	D	E	T	Ü	H	E	B	E	H	Ü	T	E	D	I	C
H	C	I	D	E	T	Ü	H	E	H	Ü	T	E	D	I	C	H

Figure 20. DER HERR BEHUTE DICH.

193. Are amulets written only on parchment?

No. Precious stones, golden plates, silver and other metals, chains, rings, etc., are also employed and engraved with the name of God or formulas as ascribed above. See Figure 21 on page 64.

194. What is the difference in result between the amulets and the spoken Schêm?

The working of the amulet is generally[19] constant and lasting, that of the pronouncing of the "Name" is of short duration but more powerful. Furthermore the working of amulets is mostly negative and averting, whereas the spoken formula is mostly productive, creative, and evoking.

---

[19]Some are also active at specific critical moments, especially "the shield of David" during a fire or (in combination with other Kabbalistic formulas) difficult deliveries, etc.

195. How much of these magical formulas and facts can be believed?

A number of the so-called miracles, like for instance the raising of the dead, belong to the world of fairy tales, while others are fantastic exaggerations of simple incidents. The statements on human-like creatures undoubtedly refer to automatons having a human form; this is especially remembered in the case of Löw's Gôlem (see question 182) since Löw was at the same time an excellent astronomer, mechanic, and physicist. The appearance of the patriarchs and that of the Hradschin (see question 182) in his study was probably brought about with the aid of the laterna magica (magic lantern). All other stories, including the creation of a Sabbath calf, are based upon self-suggestion or suggestive influence on others, like the "miracles" of the Indian fakirs, etc. This is also the case when the Kabbalist himself believes he is levitating or suggests this to others. Very powerful and more common is the suggestive influence in conjurations.

196. Were these suggestive powers known in very early times?

More so than now. A great number of the "miracles" of antiquity which have been proven to be facts (the curing of diseases, damnations, etc.) are based on this.

197. How is it proven that Kabbalism was familiar with the power of suggestion?

The Kabbalistic writing *Hechaloth rabbathi,* referred to in questions 3 and 15, extensively describes the means for self-hypnosis by use of appropriate suggestive representations, etc. To behold the secrets of the Godhead, the Kabbalist who desires this must fast on certain days, place the head between the knees while sitting, and while lying down must recite various hymns and formulas which are described. These half-sung, half-recited formulas, with their floating rhythms, pale images, and vague thoughts, are also excellent for influencing others. And finally, the Kabbalists are not ignorant of the hypnotic suggestive

Figure 21. Amulet from the works of Paracelsus.

effect of staring at a shiny object, listening to a slowly falling water, etc.[20]

198. Give an example of such a Kabbalistic hymn.

In the ninth chapter of *Hechaloth rabbathi* it is stated: "Like the voice of the water in the rustling of storms, like the voice of the waves in the blue lake while playing with the southern winds in spring, so sounds the voice of the song of praise to the throne of glory praising the king of kings. A chant of tones, a mighty roar, for many voices together form a chorus to the hymn to the throne of glory, to sing to the mighty Jacob, and from a thousand voices it reverberates upward: 'Holy, holy, holy is the Lord God of innumerable hosts!' "

199. What else belongs to Kabbalistic magic?

Astrology, physiognomy (the art of judging character from the features of the face), and chiromancy (palmistry). The magical discovery of treasures, sources, lost objects, thieves, etc., as well as dream interpretation, which all belong to lower magic and only came about in later times, have very little to do with actual Kabbalism and are more germane to popular belief.

200. Who prided himself on being an expert on secret physiognomy?

Isaac Lurja (see question 63), who stated that he could, by the features of a man, read whether his soul had transmigrated many times.

201. What can be said about Kabbalistic chiromancy?

It is not very much different from the old medieval palmistry. The Kabbalistic chiromancers distinguish: 1) the life line, starting between the thumb and the index finger and moving downward around the mount of Venus which, if sharply outlined, indicates long life; 2) the head line, beginning near the life line underneath the index finger and

---

[20]Chamisso used this suggestive effect very beautifully in his poem "Vetter Anselmo," in which the magician suggests to his cousin all ecclesiastical dignitaries, including the papacy, only to awaken him after a minute.

moving parallel with the heart line in the opposite direction which, if of sufficient length, indicates good digestion, joy of life, and energy; 3) the heart line, beginning underneath the little finger in the direction of the middle or index finger which, if sharply outlined, indicates strong procreative powers; 4) the Apollo line, beginning near the base of the hand of the mount of Venus and moving toward the little finger, which is also connected with the digestive system; 5) the Rascetta, meaning the first crossline underneath the palm at the joint of the wrist which, if not broken, indicates luck in all enterprises. The various sub-lines in the spaces between the main lines, the mounts underneath the fingers, etc., also have a meaning, as shown in Figure 22.

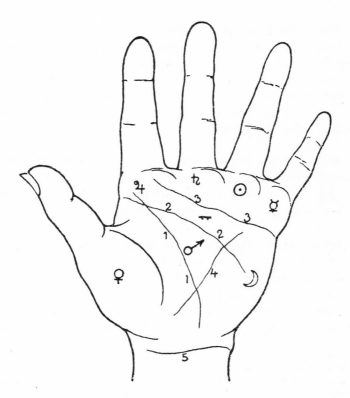

Figure 22. The chiromantic lines.

202. What does Kabbalistic astrology contain?

It corresponds with other astrology. It is based on the opinion that the stars rule man and its main goal was to read human destiny from the stars (see question 22). For this purpose the sky is divided into 12 houses (bâtthim): 1) the house of life; 2) the house of riches; 3) the house of brothers; 4) the house of relatives; 5) the house of children; 6) the house of servants; 7) the house of marital life; 8) the house of death; 9) the house of religion or compassion; 10) the house of dignities; 11) the house of friendship; 12) the house of enemies. The past and the future are determined by the position of the seven planets (Sun, Venus, Mercury, Moon, Saturn, Jupiter, and Mars) and their relation to the zodiacal signs in these houses (the casting of a person's nativity, or horoscope). The Hebrew horoscope is shown in Figure 23.

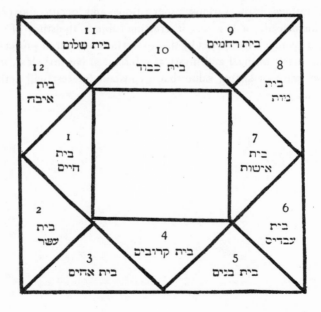

Figure 23. The twelve houses of the horoscope.

203. Did all Kabbalists engage in these activities?

No. Magical practices were peculiar to a specific direction and got the upper hand when the speculative tendency of Kabbalism slackened.

204. Is magic organically related to the fundamentals of Kabbalism?

It is not, insofar as the doctrines of Kabbalism can also exist without magic and then are even purer and nobler, whereas magic by itself is much devaluated without the nimbus of Kabbalism.

205. Give a final opinion on the Kabbala.

Speculatively viewed, it represents, although surrounded with subsidiary matter, a peculiar monism, the basic thoughts of which had an important influence on the development of later philosophy. From an ethical point of view it contains many fruitful and lofty conceptions, often shrouded in fantastic clothing. Concerning magic, it had considerable influence on various superstitious and occult movements. Socio-historically, it is a very interesting subject, the study of which, however, is much hampered by the mysterious manner of presentation and the many magical and mystical references. Nevertheless, it contains so much of lasting value that a constant interest will definitely fall to its lot.

SPECIAL NOTES

Note to Question 23. To get acquainted with the high ethical views of both Kabbalists, we quote the following from their works:

1. From Juda ben Samuel's *Book of the Pious.* "Cheat no one intentionally by your acts, also no non-Jew; do not search for dispute with others, also not with the unreligious. Be honest in your trade; do not say that one has already offered you more for your goods when this is not so; do not act as if you want to sell when you are not serious; such things are unworthy of an Israelite."

"On the money of minters, usurers, and of those cheating others in their trade with measurements and weights rests no blessing; their children and assistants will be reduced to beggary."

"If you are cheated, robbed, or slandered do not out of vengeance repay by doing the same."

"Do not speak when you are reviled, neither allow your pupils nor inmates to taunt or strike your insulter. Let envy and hatred be far from you! In case one has taxed you above your property so that the rich pay less, incite not yourself or others by protests, disputes, and anxiety but be silent and keep yourself occupied with God's Word."

2. From Eleasar ben Juda's *Rokeach:* Maintain peace in the city and outside, for all peaceful will fare well. Be sincere, do not waylay anyone by hypocrisy, cunning words, or lies. When a man lies he will die before his time; God the Lord is a God of truth, the truth is the A of creation. Be silent out of devotion, for the one who speaks much sins much. But if you speak, speak the truth, do not praise yourself but be modest."

"The humble searches to avoid marks of honor. If spoken to about his defaults, so he thanks God that he was by this reprimand given the means to better himself. If conscious of his virtues, he holds them for imperfect against the moral ideal and therefore forgives the one who slanders him."

Note to Question 32. From Mose ben Nachman's introduction to *The First Book of Moses:* "As true tradition (Kabbala) we know furthermore that the complete *Pentateuch* (The Five Books of Moses) consists only of names of God since the words can be joined in another way than the text suggests to represent God's name. Suppose the first verse of *The First Book of Moses* is read that way, then new words originate forming the name of God. This is true for the entire *Pentateuch* and the meanings based on Themerah and Gematria (see question 35) can also be added. For this reason, a copy of the *Pentateuch* in which there is one letter too many or too little is virtually unfit for use. The divine original copy was apparently written in words without sections so that one could read the letters as representing the names of God as well as interpreting them as teachings and commandment as we usually do. Moses received the laws drawn from the letter interpretation in writing, the former only orally."

Note to Question 37. Related to this is the cipher-oracle with which one calculates in advance important years and days in human life from the numbers of names and dates of birth. It is a sort of arithmetical nativity (see question 202). Emperor Wilhelm I, for instance, was born on the 22nd of the 3rd month in 1797; 22 + 3 + 1797 + 7 (the number of letters of his name) is 1829, the year of his marriage; 1829 + 1 + 8 + 2 + 9 is 1849, the Baden campaign; 1849 + 1 + 8 + 4 + 9 is 1871, his coronation as emperor; 1871 + 1 + 8 + 7 + 1 is 1888, the year of his death. Napoleon III was born on the 20th of the 4th month in 1808 or 20 + 4 + 1808 + 8 (number of letters of his name) is 1840, the rebellion in Boulogne; 1840 + 1 + 8 + 4 + 0 is 1853, his first year as emperor; 1853 + 1 + 8 + 5 + 3 is 1870, the end of his reign. Frederik Wilhelm III was married in 1793; + the sum of the numbers is 1813 (war of independence) + the sum of the numbers 13 is 1826 + (ditto) 17 is 1843 + (ditto) 16 is 1859 (the birth of Wilhelm II) + (ditto) 23 is 1882 (the birth of Crown Prince Friederich Wilhelm), etc. A sort of inverse Gematria is the effort to form words from cipher letters mainly with Roman numerals. The year of the great famine in 1315 was indicated by the following hexameter: Ut lateat nullum tempus famis, ecce CVCVLLVM. (Roman numeral M is 1000, CC is 200, LL is 100, VVV is 15; the total is 1315.)

Note to Question 44. From Gikatilla's *Schaare Orah:* "Know that all holy names of God that occur in the holy scriptures depend on the four letters that form in Hebrew the word 'Jahwe.' All other names of the Holy God are branches and twigs that sprout from the stem of the tree, each in its own way, bringing forth fruit according to its nature. Besides the famous name there are numerous secondary indications which depend on it; to 'Jahwe,' for instance, belong the denominations: the terrible, forgiver of sin, destroyer of crime; to 'El' (God): the great, the charitable, the merciful; to 'Elohim' (Godhead): the powerful, the judge, the lord of justice. To all these surnames belong again names depending on them, and they are the total of other words of the holy scripture."

Note to Question 45. Abraham Zakkuto cites in his book *Juchasin* (Chronical, written in 1504) the following from *Meirath enajim* (about 1300): "In Valladolid I met Rabbi Mose de Leon who assured me under oath that he was in the possession of the original of the *Zohar* by Rabbi Simeon ben Yohai. It was at his home in Avila and he wanted to show it to me. On the way back he died (1305) at Arevalo. In Avila I enjoyed the hospitality of the old scholar Rabbi David Raphan, a relative of Mose de Leon. I urgently requested him to inform me about the authenticity of the *Zohar*. He told me that as far as he was concerned it was certain that Rabbi Mose had invented the book himself. His motive for this was the fact that Mose had often sent writings of mysterious and peculiar content to rich people in the surroundings for a high price. He immediately spent the money. He died without leaving a penny so that his wife and children were in great want. When I heard of his death I immediately went to Rabbi Jozef de Avila who was very rich and had often given him presents; I said to him: 'This is a good moment for you to obtain the beautiful book (the *Zohar* from which Rabbi Mose de Leon pretended to have copied his statements) for a good price from his widow.' When they offered the widow a large sum of money she swore that her husband had never possessed such a book but that everything came out of his own mind. When she had once asked him why he ascribed his work to someone else and whether it would not be better if he made himself known as the author, he answered that if he published it as his own work, no one would appreciate it and therefore would not pay much for it; therefore he had ascribed it to Rabbi Simeon ben Yohai and his followers. Later (Rabbi Isaac continues) I talked with his daughter who made a similar statement."

In spite of all this, one has for a long time held the opinion that Simeon ben Yohai was the author and Knorr van Rosenroth (*Kaballa denudata* II, page 5) also defends this assertion.

Note to Question 46. From the introduction to the *Zohar* (Volume I, 15A): "In the beginning the decision of the king (the Godhead) made a tracing in the supernal effulgence of a lamp of scintillation, and there issued within the impenetrable recesses of the mysterious limitless a shapeless nucleus enclosed in a ring neither white nor black nor red nor green nor of any color at all. When he took measurements, he fashioned colors to show within, and within the lamp there issued a certain effluence from which colors were imprinted below. The most mysterious power enshrouded in the limitless remaining clave, as it were, without cleaving its void, wholly unknowable until from the force of the strokes there shone forth a supernal and mysterious point. Beyond that point there is no knowable, and therefore it is called Reschith (beginning), the creative utterance which is the starting point of all."

Note to Question 63. Rabbi Isaac Lurja was born in Palestine in 1534. After the early death of his father, his mother left with the 16-year-old boy to go to her brother in Egypt, who was a toll collector and who later gave his daughter in marriage to Rabbi Isaac. After twenty years in Egypt he went to Safed in Palestine where the former pupil of Kordovero (see question 60), Chajjim Vidal, became his disciple. "In the thirty-eighth year of his life," states the book *Emek hamelech* (see question 71) "he was called from here (Zapeth) to the high academy because of our many sins."

Note to Question 75. Jonathan Eibeschütz was born in 1690 in Krakow. After being educated as a Talmudist by Rabbi Meir Eisenstadt (Worms) and his father-in-law Rabbi Isaac Spiro, he became a rabbi in Jungbunzlau in Boheme when he was twelve years old. Soon after, Eibeschütz moved to Prague where he became famous and stayed until 1740. In 1750 after ten years' work in Metz he was offered the rabbinate of the three parishes of Altona, Hamburg, and Wandsbech. It was here that the grim fight between he and his colleague Emden from Altona began, which divided almost all of European Judaism into two hostile camps. Eibeschütz had written several amulets wherein his opponents discovered traces of Sabbathairian heresy, while he and his followers represented them as free from such. Practically all Jewish authorities acted as arbitrators for both parties and many made judgments only to reverse them later. The king of Denmark, as sovereign lord, also wished the opinion of the Christian scholars but even these were far from unanimous—some even labeled Eibeshütz as a disguised Christian. The king, who was uneasy about the matter, alternately decided in favor of one or the other party, and when Eibeschütz died in 1764, the fight had not yet ended. In his preachings, Eibeschütz often cited the *Zohar* as well as various modern Talmud scholars. His commentaries to *Schulchan aruch* are also famous.

In the 18th century the Frankists (Zoharists, contra-Talmudists) played an important role among the followers of the Kabbala and especially of the *Zohar*. They were followers of the famous Polish Jacob Frank, who was born in 1719 and who died in great esteem and riches in 1791 in Offenbach.

Note to Question 78. It is remarkable that up until far into the 19th century Kabbalism had many convinced adherents among the Catholic priests (especially in Austria).

Note to Question 79. Johannes Reuchlin, the famous humanist and advocate of reformation, an uncle of Melanchton, was born on the 28th of December 1455 in Pforzheim. After he had studied Greek and Latin in Paris in 1473 he taught ancient languages at The University of Basel from 1474-1478 and continued in Orleans after 1478. He also studied law there. In 1481 he taught jurisprudence and literature in Tubingen where he had a law practice. He became a favorite of Duke Eberhard, with whom he visited Italy where his knowledge of the Greek language was highly prized. After carrying out several important missions for the duke he returned to Italy in 1490 and learned Hebrew from Leone da Modena, a study which he continued with the Jewish personal physician of Emperor Maximilian, Jechiel Loans. In 1494 he wrote his Kabbalistic book *De verbo mirifico*. In 1509 Maximillian ordered all Hebrew writings burned and Reuchlin, when asked for his opinion, protested heavily, which resulted in the famous struggle with the Dominicans from Cologne and their sham, the baptized Jew Pfefferkorn. Reuchlin incurred a trial from the Inquisition which he, however, won in spite of the verdicts of the universities of Paris, Erfurts and Mainz. The most famous verdict resulted from the dispute of the "Obscure letters" (Epistolae obscurorum vigorum) published by his followers (Ulrich von Huten, Conrad Celtes, Willibald Pirkeimer and others), wherein his opponents are rightly mocked. Reuchlin died in Stuttgart on the 30th of June 1522. Among the orthodox Christian Hebrew scholars he was, however, not very popular.

Note to Question 85. The assumption that the *Zohar* teaches a blood ritual is based on the misinterpretation of many mysterious allegorically intended passages where misfortune and suffering are compared to slaughter (for instance in the *Tikunê Zohar*, *Zohar Chadasch* Vol. II, 57). The foolishness of this allegory had its revenge 500 years late when this passage was considered the fundamental doctrine for a blood ritual although not corresponding to it in the least.

Note to Question 152. Compare the scholarly study of Felix Laudowicz: *Essence and Origin of the Doctrines of Pre-existence and Transmigration of Souls* (Leipzig, G. Fock, 1898).

Note to Question 155. Compare Olcott, *Buddhistic Catechism.*

Note to Question 164. Regarding transmigration see the following:

1. *First Book of Moses* (Chapter 3 verse 16): "Til thou return unto the ground, for out of it was thou taken" (according to the Hebrew text), "from where thou comest." This should indicate a renewed incarnation!

2. *Fifth Book of Moses* (Chapter 33 verse 6): According to the Aramaic translation: "Ruben lives and dies no second death."

3. *Ecclesiastes* (Chapter 4 verse 9): "One generation passeth away and another generation cometh—the king that hath been it is that which shall be."

4. *Ecclesiastes* (Chapter 8 verse 10): "And so I saw the wicked buried who had come and gone from the place of the holy." (In Hebrew "come" is "come again.")

5. *Second Book of Samuel* (Chapter 14 verse 14): "Neither does God respect any person, yet doth he devise means that his banished be not expelled from him."

6. *Job* (Chapter 1 verse 21): "Naked came I out of my mother's womb and naked shall I return thither." Namely (according to Kabbalistic conception), in a renewed birth.

Note to Question 176. Compare S. Krauss, *The Life of Jesus According to Jewish Data* (Berlin 1902).

Note to Question 195. See Olcott, *Buddhistic Catechism*, p.p. 352-363.

Note to Question 199. An authentic Chaldean (meaning Aramaic) dream book exists within the Talmudic tract *Berachoth*.

Note to Question 201. In the beginning of the 18th century most German universities still had lectures on palmistry; for instance, in Jena be Professor Hexner and in Holland by Professor Nietzky.

Note to Question 202. In the beginning of the 19th century a German professor defended astrology (J.W. Pfaff, *Astrology*, Bamburg, 1816 and *About Planetary Conjunctions in the Star of Bethlehem*, Bamburg, 1812).

Note to Question 204. In order to rectify a widespread error I would decidedly like to state that additional work such as *The Sixth and Seventh Book of Moses* or *The Secrets of the Kabbala* have absolutely nothing to do with Kabbalism but are pure nonsense being sold for extremely high prices.